The Silly Little Book

of

SMELLY

JOKES

The Silly Little Book
of
SMELLY
JOKES

This is a Parragon Book

This edition published in 2002

Parragon
Queen Street House
4 Queen Street
Bath BA1 1HE, UK

Produced by Magpie Books an imprint of
Robinson Publishing Ltd, London

Hardback   ISBN 0-75258-628-9
Paperback ISBN 0-75258-636-X

A copy of the British Library Cataloguing-in-Publication Data
is available from the British Library

Printed and bound in China

Contents

Introduction

We've all whiffed a few smelly things, and some people more than others! But judging by the hilarious jokes in these "phew" pages, the world out there is a lot smellier than we thought! So read on and take advice from vampires for curing bad breath (they use extractor fangs), or if your problem is smelly ears, learn how best to clean them (eat a large watermelon!)

Just Plain Smelly

Two little girls were paddling on the beach. Nicky said, "Coo! Aren't your feet mucky?"

Sticky looked down at her feet. "They are a bit," she replied, "but you see, we didn't come last year."

What do you call a dirty, frayed, hairy, blood-stained thing found on the bathroom floor?

A used Elastoplast.

What did one eye say to the other?
"Between us is something that
smells."

Who wrote a treatise on
seasickness?
Eva Lott.

What does the Queen do when
she belches?
Issues a royal pardon.

Knock, knock,
Who's there?
Why?
Why who?
Why pa your nose, it's dripping.

Knock, knock.
Who's there.
Few.
Few who?
Phew! There's an awful smell
round here, is it you?

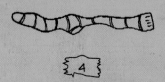

Is that perfume I smell?
It is and you do.

Who is the smelliest, hairiest
monarch in the world?
King Pong.

How do vampires keep their breath
smelling nice?
They use extractor fangs.

What's the difference between a huge, ugly, smelly monster and a sweet?
People like sweets.

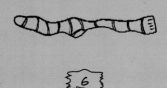

Ding dong bell,
Pussy's down the well,
But we've put some disinfectant down
And don't mind about the smell.

First Witch: What's your new boyfriend like?
Second Witch: He's mean, nasty, ugly, smelly, and totally evil – but he has some bad points too.

Did you hear about the stupid man who thought that "the great smell of Brut" was King Kong's B.O.?

Doctor, doctor, I've got bad teeth, foul breath and smelly feet.
Sounds like you've got foot and mouth disease.

What do you get if you cross a tarantula with a rose?
I don't know but I wouldn't try smelling one.

A wizard went to the doctor one day complaining of headaches. "It's because I live in the same room as two of my brothers," he said. "One of them has six goats and the other has four pigs and they all live in the room with us. The smell is terrible."

"Well couldn't you just open the windows?" asked the doctor.

"Certainly not," he replied, "my bats would fly out."

What do you get if you cross a
man-eating monster with a skunk?
A very ugly smell.

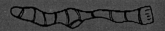

"Mary," said her teacher, "you
can't bring that lamb into school.
What about the smell?"
"Oh, that's all right Miss," said
Mary. "It'll soon get used to it."

Ben, sniffing: Smells like UFO for dinner tonight, chaps.
Ken: What's UFO?
Ben: Unidentified Frying Objects.

Did you hear about the horrible, hairy monster who did farmyard impressions?
He didn't do the noises, he just made the smells.

What do you get if you cross a skunk and an owl?
A bird that smells but doesn't give a hoot!

"What's your new perfume called?" a young man asked his girlfriend.
"High Heaven," she replied.
"I asked what it was called, not what it smells to!"

Which soldiers smell of salt and pepper?
Seasoned troopers.

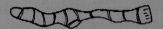

"There's a dreadful smell of B.O. in here," said the new office boy.
"It's the automatic air conditioning," said his boss.
"Automatic air conditioning?"
"Whenever the weather gets hot it automatically breaks down!"

A man with B.O. walked into a drugstore and said, "I'd like something to take this smell away."
"So would I, Sir" said the druggist. "So would I."

Did you hear about the new prize for people who cure themselves of B.O.?
It's called the No-Smell Prize.

What dog smells of onions?
A hot dog.

"Ugh! You smell terrible," said a
doctor to a patient.
"That's odd," said the patient.
"That's what the other doctor
said."
"If you were told that by another
doctor, why have you come to me?"
"Because I wanted a second
opinion."

Doctor, doctor, my friend told me I had B.O.
And what makes you think he's right, you disgusting, smelly, malodorous, foul, little man?

What lies on the ground 100 feet up in the air and smells?
A dead centipede.

What's wet, smells and goes ba-bump, ba-bump?
A skunk in the spin-drier.

Jane: Have you noticed that your mother smells a bit funny these days?

Wayne: No. Why?

Jane: Well your sister told me she was giving her a bottle of toilet water for her birthday.

Knock, knock.
Who's there?
Sonia.
Sonia who?
Sonia shoe. I can smell it from here.

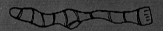

What's the smelliest city in America?
Phew York.

"Keep that dog out of my garden. It smells disgusting!" a neighbor said to a small boy one day.
The boy went home to tell everyone to stay away from the neighbor's garden because of the smell!

Have you heard about the new aftershave that drives women crazy?
No! Tell me about it.
It smells of fifty-dollar notes.

What do you get if you cross a crocodile with a flower?
I don't know, but I'm not going to smell it.

What smells of fish and goes round and round at 100 miles an hour?
A goldfish in a blender.

Doctor, doctor, my husband smells like a fish.
Poor sole!

Doctor, doctor, I've had tummy ache since I ate three crabs yesterday.
Did they smell bad when you took them out of their shells?
What do you mean "took them out of their shells"?

How can you tell if an elephant has been sleeping in your bed?
The sheets are wrinkled and the bed smells of peanuts.

Knock, knock.
Who's there?
Hali.
Hali who?
Halitosis – your breath smells
awful!

Darren: I'm so tired I feel like an
old sock.
Sharon: I thought there was a
funny smell in here!

Personal
Pongs

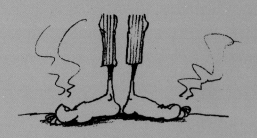

Who wrote *Smelly Socks and Dirty Feet?*
I. Malone.

Two dentists were discussing a patient.
Mr Phang said, "I wouldn't say his teeth were rotten, but every time he stuck his tongue out one of them snapped off."

Melissa had been given a recorder and a bottle of perfume for her birthday. Her parents had invited some friends round to celebrate, and, as they sat down for tea, Melissa smiled shyly and said to one of her mother's friends, "If you hear a little noise, and smell a little smell, its me."

Mrs Toe-Rag: Ophelia! Wash your hands before you play the piano!
Ophelia: But Mom, I only play on the black notes.

Jenny: I think my brother's built upside-down.
Penny: How's that?
Jenny: His nose runs and his feet smell.

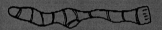

What did the secretary do with old fingernails?
File them.

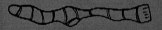

How do you catch dandruff?
Brush your hair over a paper bag.

Knock, knock.
Who's there?
Colleen.
Colleen who?
Colleen yourself up, you look filthy.

What kind of monster can sit on
the end of your finger?
A bogeyman.

What's the difference between a dead dog and a musician? One composes and the other decomposes.

Why did the idiot burn his ear? Someone phoned him while he was ironing.

Doctor, doctor, my kidneys are bad. What should I do? Take them back to the butcher's.

Stinker was riding his bike round the block faster and faster, showing off to his friends. With each round he became more daring. First of all he rode round shouting, "Look, no hands!" Then he rode round shouting, "Look, no feet!" The third time he came round he mumbled, "Look, no teeth!"

Stinker was climbing a tree and had nearly reached the top when his mother came into the garden and saw him. She shouted up, "If you fall and break both legs, don't come running to me, that's all."

Who is the meanest person in the world?
A man who finds a sling and then breaks his arm to wear it.

Why did his friends call Edgar
"Camembert"?
They were cheesed of by the smell
of his feet.

Mother: Harold! What did you say
to Bessie to make her cry?
Harold: I paid her a compliment.
Mother: And what was that?
Harold: I told her she sweated less
than any girl I'd ever danced with.

What happened when two fat men ran in a race?
One ran in short bursts, the other ran in burst shorts.

When a photographer took Boris's photograph he never developed it. He was afraid of being alone in the dark with it.

Knock, knock.
Who's there?
Philippa.
Philippa who?
Philippa bath, I'm very dirty.

Audrey: Do you always bathe in muddy water?
Tawdry: It wasn't muddy when I got in.

Bertha: My sister can play the piano by ear.
Basil: So what? My brother fiddles with his toes.

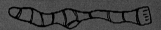

Mrs Slack: This tea is terrible.
Mr Slack: I made it in my pyjamas.
Mrs Slack: No wonder it tastes so bad.

Stinker: I live on garlic alone.
Pongo: Anyone who lives on garlic should live alone.

Why can't a steam engine sit down?
Because it has a tender behind.

When can't you bury people who live opposite a graveyard?
When they're not dead.

What were Batman and Robin called after they'd been run over by a steamroller?
Flatman and Ribbon.

What was proved when the fat man
was run over by a steamroller?
That he had a lot of guts.

What happened when Lucy pushed
her father's fingers in the light
socket?
She got fizzy pop.

When do you get that run-down
feeling?
When you've been hit by a car.

How can you make a thin person fat?
Push him over a cliff and he'll come down plump.

Why did the man jump off the top of the Empire State Building?
Because he wanted to make a hit on Broadway.

What do you do if you laugh until your sides split?
Run until you get a stitch.

Why do frogs have webbed feet?
To stamp out forest fires.

Why did King Kong paint the
bottoms of his feet brown?
So that he could hide upside down
in a jar of peanut butter.

What do you give a monster with
big feet?
Big flippers.

If a crocodile makes shoes, what does a banana make?
Slippers.

Why shouldn't you dance with a Yeti?
Because if it trod on you you might get flat feet.

Why should men be careful of beautiful witches?
They'll sweep them off their feet.

How do you know a zombie is tired?
He's dead on his feet.

First Witch: I'm going to cast a
spell and make myself beautiful.
I'll have hundreds of men at my
feet.
Second witch: Yes, chiropodists.

Centipede: Doctor, doctor, when my
feet hurt, I hurt all over.

Why do spiders enjoy swimming?
They have webbed feet.

"Lie flat on your backs, class, and circle your feet in the air as if you were riding your bikes," said the gym teacher.
"Alec! What are you doing. Move your feet boy."
"I'm freewheeling, Sir."

"Ann," said the dancing mistress. "There are two things stopping you becoming the world's greatest ballerina?"

"What are they, Miss?" asked Ann.

"Your feet."

What do you call an English teacher, five feet tall, covered from head to toe in boils and totally bald?
Sir!

Can you stand on your head?
I've tried, but I can't get my feet up high enough.

What has eight feet and sings?
The school quartet.

We're so poor that mum and dad can't afford to buy me shoes. I have to blacken my feet and lace my toes together.

Chuck: Do you have holes in your underpants?
Teacher: No, of course not.
Chuck: Then how do you get your feet through?

What has two heads, three hands,
two noses and five smelly feet?
A monster with spare parts.

Why did the teacher marry the
school cleaner?
Because she swept him off his
feet.

Two monsters were in hospital and they were discussing their operations and ailments.
"Have you had your feet checked?" one asked the other.
"No," came the reply. "They've always been purple with green spots."

How can you drop a bad egg six feet without breaking it?
By dropping it seven feet – it won't break for the first six.

Robot: I have to dry my feet
carefully after a bath.
Monster: Why?
Robot: Otherwise I get rusty nails.

Doctor, doctor, I can't stand being
three feet tall any longer.
Then you'll just have to learn to be
a little patient.

How do ghosts keep their feet
dry?
By wearing boo-ts.

Dotty Aunt Muriel received a letter one morning, and upon reading it burst into floods of tears.

"What's the matter?" asked her companion.

"Oh dear," sobbed Auntie. "It's my favorite nephew. He's got three feet."

"Three feet?" exclaimed her friend. "Surely that's not possible?"

"Well," said Auntie, "his mother's just written to tell me he's grown another foot!"

Joan, pick up your feet when you walk.
What for, mom? I've only got to put them down again.

Why do bees have sticky hair?
Because they have honey combs.

What has webbed feet and fangs?
Count Quackula.

"If you're going to work here, young man," said the boss, "one thing you must learn is that we are very keen on cleanliness in this firm. Did you wipe your feet on the mat as you came in?"

"Oh, yes sir."

"And another thing, we are very keen on truthfulness. There is no mat."

What's thick, black, floats on water and shouts "Knickers"?
Crude oil.

Teacher: You're wearing a very strange pair of socks, Darren. One's blue with red spots, and one's yellow with green stripes.
Darren: Yes, and I've got another pair just the same at home.

How do monsters count to 13?
On their fingers.
How do they count to 47?
They take off their smelly socks and count their toes.

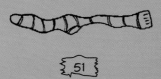

You've got your socks on inside out.
I know, Mom, but there are holes on the other side.

What do you get if you cross an ant with half a pair of knickers?
Pant.

Why do elephants have flat feet?
From jumping out of tall trees.

One very hot day an extremely small man went into a café, put his newspaper on a table and went to the counter. But on returning with a cup of tea he saw that his place had been taken by a stinking, bearded, ferocious-looking man of some 300 pounds in weight, and six feet nine inches in height.

"Excuse me," said the little man to the big man, "but you're sitting in my seat."

"Oh yeah?" snarled the big man. "Prove it!"

"Certainly. You're sitting on my ice-cream."

Andy was late for school.
"Andy!" roared his mother. "Have you got your socks on yet?"
"Yes, Mom," replied Andy. "All except one."

Cherry: What's Cheryl like?
Jerry: She's a slick chick.
Cherry: You mean she's like a greasy chicken?

How do you survive the electric chair?
Insulate your underpants.

If a dog is tied to a rope 15 feet long, how can it reach a smelly bone 30 feet away?
The rope isn't tied to anything!

Animal
Aromas

What's black and white, and goes moo, moo, splat?
A cow falling over a cliff.

Two policemen in New York were watching King Kong climb up the Empire State Building. One said to the other, "What do you think he's doing?"
"It's obvious," replied his colleague, "he wants to catch a plane."

What do you get if you cross a frog
with a decathelete?
Someone who pole vaults without a
pole.

How do you catch a squirrel?
Climb up a tree and act like a nut.

Did you hear about the boy who
was told to do 100 lines?
He drew 100 cats on the paper.
He thought the teacher had said
lions.

Two caterpillars were crawling along a twig when a butterfly flew by.
"You know," said one caterpillar to the other, "when I grow up, you'll never get me in one of those things.

What do you get if you cross a snake with a hotdog?
A fangfurther.

What do you get if you cross King Kong with a watchdog?
A terrified postman.

"Waiter, this food isn't fit for a pig!"
"All right, I'll get you some that is."

What do you get if you cross a snake with a pig?
A boar constrictor.

What happened when the nasty
monster stole a pig?
The pig squealed to the police.

Why was the centipede late?
Because she was playing "this
Little Piggy" with her baby.

Why couldn't the vulture talk to the
dove?
Because he didn't speak pigeon
English.

What did the neurotic pig say to the farmer?
You take me for grunted.

Doctor, doctor, I've got a little sty.
Then you'd better buy a little pig.

Why did the teacher put corn in his shoes?
Because he had pigeon toes.

Why did the pig run away from the pigsty?
He felt that the other pigs were taking him for grunted.

What do you call a multi story pigpen?
A styscraper.

Father: You eat like a pig, Edward. Do you know what a pig is?
Edward: Yes, a hog's son.

What do you get if you cross a bee with a skunk?
A creature that stinks and stings.

Peggy: I've just come back from the beauty parlor.
Piggy: Pity it was closed!

What do you get if you cross an octopus with a skunk?
An octopong.

Mary: Do you think my sister's pretty?
Gary: Well, let's just say if you pulled her pigtail she'd probably say "oink, oink"!

What would you get if you crossed
King Kong with a skunk?
I don't know but it could always get
a seat on a bus!

How many skunks does it take to
make a big stink?
A phew!

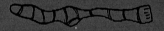

What do you get if you cross a
jellyfish with a sheepdog?
Colliewobbles.

Baby Skunk: But, Mom, why can't I have a chemistry set for my birthday?

Mother: Because it would stink the house out, that's why.

"Please Miss!" said a little boy at kindergarten. "We're going to play elephants and circuses, do you want to join in?"

"I'd love to," said the teacher. "What do you want me to do?"

"You can be the lady that feeds us peanuts!"

Three animals were having a drink in a café, when the owner asked for the money. "I'm not paying," said the duck. "I've only got one bill and I'm not breaking it."

"I've spent my last buck," said the deer.

"Then the duck'll have to pay," said the skunk. "Getting here cost me my last scent."

What happened to the vampire who swallowed a sheep?
He felt baaaaaaaaaaaaad.

What happens if you cross a
werewolf with a sheep?
You have to get a new sheep.

The Stock Market is a place where
sheep and cattle are sold.

What do you get if you cross a
sheep dog and a bunch of
daisies?
Collie flowers!

What do you get if you cross a
sheep and a rainstorm?
A wet blanket.

Mr Butcher, have you got a sheep's
head?
No, madam, it's just the way I part
my hair.

Why are skunks always arguing?
'Cos they like to raise a stink.

Doctor, doctor, I've just been sprayed by a skunk. Should I put some cream on it?
Well you could. But I doubt if you'll be able to catch it.

What's black and white, pongs and hangs from a line?
A drip-dry skunk.

What do you get if you cross an eagle with a skunk?
A bird that stinks to high heaven.

What do you get if you cross an
elephant with some locusts?
I'm not sure, but if they ever swarm
– watch out!

What do you get if you cross a
worm with an elephant?
Big holes in your garden.

Why do elephants have trunks?
Because they don't have glove
compartments.

Why doesn't Kermit like
elephants?
They always want to play leap frog
with him.

How can you prevent an elephant
from charging?
Take away his credit card.

Tom: What did the banana say to
the elephant?
Nik: I don't know.
Tom: Nothing. Bananas can't talk.

What is Smokey the Elephant's middle name?
The.

Why did the elephant put his trunk across the trail?
To trip up the ants.

What do you get if you cross an elephant with a spider?
I don't know but if it crawled over your ceiling the house would collapse.

What do you get if you cross an elephant with the abominable snowman?
A jumbo yeti.

"Why are you tearing up your homework notebook and scattering the pieces around the playground?" a furious teacher asked one of her pupils.
"To keep the elephants away, Miss."
"There are no elephants."
"Shows how effective it is then, doesn't it?"

What's the best thing to give a
seasick elephant?
Plenty of room.

Which animals were the last to
leave the ark?
The elephants – they were packing
their trunks.

Anna: I was top of the class last week.

Mom: How did you manage that?

Anna: I managed to answer a question about elephants.

Mom: What question?

Anna: Well, the teacher asked us how many legs an elephant had, and I said five.

Mom: But that wasn't right.

Anna: I know, but it was the nearest anyone got.

Why did the elephant paint her head yellow?
To see if blondes really do have more fun.

What do you get if you cross a caretaker with an elephant?
A twenty-ton school cleaner.

My dad is so shortsighted he can't get to sleep unless he counts elephants.

Did you hear about the ogre who threw trunks over cliffs?
Nothing special about that, you might think – but the elephants were still attached.

What do you get if you cross an elephant and peanut butter?
Either peanut butter that never forgets, or an elephant that sticks to the roof of your mouth.

An elephant ran away from a circus and ended up in a little old lady's back garden. Now she had never seen an elephant before, so she rang the police.

"Please come quickly," she said to the policeman who answered the phone. "There's a strange looking animal in my garden picking up cabbages with its tail."

"What's it doing with them?" asked the policeman.

"If I told you," said the old lady, "you'd never believe me!"

What did the grape do when the elephant sat on it?
It let out a little wine.

How does an elephant go up a tree?
It stands on an acorn and waits for it to grow.

Why did the elephant cross the road?
To pick up the flattened chicken.

Is the squirt from
trunk very powerful
Of course – a jumbo
500 people in the air f
time.

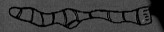

Visitor: Wow, you have a lot of f
buzzing round your horses and
cows. Do you ever shoo them?
Rancher: No, we just let them go
barefoot.

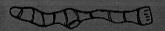

How do you make an elephant
sandwich?
First of all you get a very large
loaf . . .

What happened when the ghostly
cows got out of their field?
There was udder chaos.

Teacher: Name six things that
contain milk.
Daft Dora: Custard, cocoa, and
four cows.

Dim Dinah wrote in her exercise book: Margarine is butter made from imitation cows.

Dad, when I get old will the calves of my legs be cows . . .?

What is cowhide most used for? Holding cows together.

What do you get it you cross a
hedgehog with a giraffe?
A long-necked toothbrush.

What do we get from naughty
cows?
Bad milk!

Dad, is an ox a sort of male cow?
Sort of, yes.
And equine means something to
do with horses, doesn't it?
That's right.
So what's an equinox?

Joe: Did you ever see a horse fly?
Pete: No, but I once saw a cow
jump off a cliff.

Did you hear about the headless horseman who got a job in a department store?
He's the head buyer.

What would happen if tarantulas were as big as horses?
If one bit you, you could ride it to hospital.

"What did the doctor say to you yesterday?" asked the teacher.
"He said I was allergic to horses."
"I've never heard of anyone suffering from that. What's the condition called?"
"Bronco-itis."

When my girlfriend goes out riding, she looks like part of the horse.
When she dismounts, she still looks like part of the horse.

This morning I felt that today was going to be my lucky day. I got up at seven, had seven dollars in my pocket, there were seven of us at lunch and there were seven horses in the seven o'clock race – so I backed the seventh.
Did it win?
No, it came seventh.

Why was Dracula so happy at the races?
His horse won by a neck.

Did you hear about the stupid
water polo player?
His horse drowned . . .

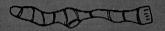

A mean horseman went into a
saddler's shop and asked for one
spur.
"One spur?" asked the saddler.
"Surely you mean a pair of spurs,
sir?"
"No, just one," replied the
horseman. "If I can get one side of
the horse to go, the other side is
bound to come with it!"

The swing doors of the Wild West saloon crashed open and in came Little Pete, black with fury. "All right!" he raged. "All right! Who did it? What goddarned varmint painted my horse blue?"

And the huge figure of Smelly Jake, notorious gunfighter and town baddie rose from a chair by the door. "It was me, shrimp," he drawled, bunching his gigantic fists, "what about it?"

"Oh, well, er," stammered little Pete wretchedly, "all I wanted to say was . . . when are you going to give it another coat?"

He's so stupid he thinks Camelot is where Arabs park their camels. She's so stupid she thinks hair spray is something you use to get rid of rabbits.

Paddy went to a riding stable and hired a horse.

"Hold on for a moment," said the assistant as he helped him onto the horse, "aren't you putting that saddle on backwards?"

"You don't even know which way I want to go!"

The box office clerk at the theater went to the manager's office to tell him that there were two horses in the foyer.

"Two horses?" exclaimed the manager in surprise. "What on earth do they want?"

"Two stalls for Monday night."

Whiffy
Pets

What is pretty and delicate and
carries a submachine gun?
A killer butterfly.

Why is a frog luckier than a cat?
Because a frog croaks all the time
– a cat only croaks nine times.

What's a rat's least favorite
record?
"What's up Pussycat."

What does an educated owl say?
Whom.

What do you get if you cross a
long-fanged, purple-spotted
monster with a cat?
A town that is free of dogs.

How do you catch King Kong?
Hang upside down and make a
noise like a banana.

What do you get if you cross King
Kong with a frog?
A gorilla that catches airplanes
with its tongue.

What happened when the cannibal
got religion?
He only ate Catholics on Fridays.

What happened when a cannibal
went on a self-catering holiday?
He ate himself.

What has six legs and flies?
A witch giving her cat a lift.

Why did the witch climb Nelson's
Column?
To get her cat back.

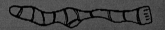

Why are black cats such good
singers?
They're very mewsical.

When it is unlucky to see a black
cat?
When you're a mouse.

What do you call it when a witch's
cat falls off her broomstick?
A catastrophe.

What do you get if you cross a cat
with Father Christmas?
Santa Claws.

How do you get milk from a witch's cat?
Steal her saucer.

What do you get if you cross a witch's cat with a canary?
A peeping tom.

What is an octopus?
An eight-sided cat.

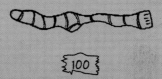

What did the black cat say to the
fish head?
I've got a bone to pick with you.

What do you call a cat that drinks
vinegar?
A sour puss.

What has four legs, a tail, whiskers
and flies?
A dead witch's cat.

What do you call a cat who never comes when she's called?
Im-puss-able.

What has four legs, a tail, whiskers and goes round and round for hours?
A black cat in a tumble drier.

What do you get if you cross a cat
and a canary?
A cat with a full tummy.

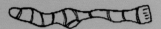

What do you call a cat with no
legs?
Anything you like – she won't be
able to come anyway.

What is a black cat's favorite TV
program?
Miami Mice.

What's furry, has whiskers and
chases outlaws?
A posse cat.

What do witches' cats strive for?
Purr-fection.

What do you call a witch's cat who
can spring from the ground to her
mistress's hat in one leap?
A good jum-purr.

What do you call a witch's cat who
can do spells as well as her
mistress?
An ex-purr-t.

A wizard who's as bald as a bat
Spilt hair tonic over the mat.
It's grown so much higher,
He can't see the fire
And he thinks that it's smothered
his cat.

What did the zombie get his
medal for?
Deadication.

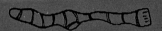

There once was a very strong cat
Who had a fight with a bat.
The bat flew away
And at the end of the day
The cat had a scrap with a rat.

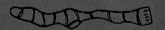

First cat: Where do fleas go in
winter?
Second cat: Search me!

Wizard: Have you put the cat out?
Witch: Was he burning again?

First Witch: See my cat? He's just drunk 83 saucers of milk.
Second Witch: That must be a lap record.

"Won't you let me live one of my own lives?" said the put-upon young cat to its parents.

First Witch: My boyfriend's gone and stolen my black cat.

Second Witch: You mean your familiar.

First Witch: Well we were, but I'm not speaking to him now.

Witch: Doctor, doctor, I keep thinking I'm my own cat.

Doctor: How long have you thought this?

Witch: Since I was a kitten.

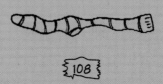

What happened to the girl who
wore a mouse costume to her
halloween party?
The cat ate her.

What did one black cat say to the
other?
Nothing. Cats can't speak.

What did the black cat do when its
tail was cut off?
It went to a re-tail store.

What do you get when a vampire
bites a rat?
A neighborhood free of cats.

What kind of cats love water?
Octopusses.

What's an American cat's favorite
car?
A Catillac.

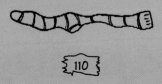

Teacher: And did you see the Catskill Mountains on your visit to America?

Jimmy: No, but I saw them kill mice.

A man out for a walk came across a little boy pulling his cat's tail. "Hey, you!" he called. "Don't pull the cat's tail!"

"I'm not pulling!" replied the little boy. "I'm only holding on – the cat's doing the pulling!"

What fish do dogs chase?
Catfish.

I went fly-fishing yesterday.
Catch anything?
Yes, a three-pound bluebottle.

This loaf is nice and warm!
It should be – the cat's been
sitting on it all day!

First cat: How did you get on in the milk drinking contest?
Second cat: Oh, I won by six laps!

Teacher: Who can tell me what "dogma" means?
Cheeky Charlie: It's a lady dog that's had puppies, Sir.

What did Dracula say to the Wolfman?
"You look like you're going to the dogs."

Why was the Abominable
Snowman's dog called Frost?
Because Frost bites.

Why was the cannibal looking
peeky?
Because he'd just eaten a
Chinese dog.

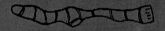

What do you call a dog owned by
Dracula?
A blood hound.

Emm: What's the name of your dog?
Nik: Ginger.
Emm: Does Ginger bite?
Nik: No, but Ginger snaps.

Mother: Keep that dog out of the house, it's full of fleas.
Son: Keep out of the house, Fido, it's full of fleas.

What did the clean dog say to the insect?
"Long time no flea!"

What's the difference between fleas and dogs?
Dogs can have fleas but fleas can't have dogs.

Why was the mother flea feeling down in the dumps?
Because she thought her children were all going to the dogs.

Two monsters went duck hunting with their dogs but without success.
"I know what we're doing wrong," said the first one.
"What's that then?" said the second.
"We're not throwing the dogs high enough!"

What did one flea say to another after a night out?
"Shall we walk home or take a dog?"

What's the difference between a flea-bitten dog and a bored visitor?
One's going to itch. The other's itching to go.

What happened to the skeleton
that was attacked by a dog?
It ran off with some bones and left
him without a leg to stand on.

What is small, furry and smells like
bacon.
A hamster.

My dog saw a sign that said: "Wet
Paint" – so he did!

My dog is a nuisance. He chases everyone on a bicycle. What can I do?

Take his bike away.

A man went into the local department store where he saw a sign on the escalator – Dogs must be carried on this escalator.

The man then spent the next two hours looking for a dog.

Why does the Hound of the Baskervilles turn round and round before he lies down for the night? Because he's the watchdog and he has to wind himself up.

Caspar: I was the teacher's pet last year.
Jaspar: Why was that?
Caspar: She couldn't afford a dog.

Teacher: What is meant by doggerel?
Terry: Little dogs, Miss.

A blind man went into a shop, picked up his dog by the tail and swung it around his head.
"Can I help you?" asked the assistant.
"No thanks," said the blind man, "I'm just looking around."

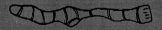

Doctor, Doctor! I think I'm a dog!
Sit down, please.
Oh no – I'm not allowed on the
furniture.

My dog plays chess.
Your dog plays chess? He must be
really clever!
Oh, I don't know. I usually beat him
three times out of four.

If twenty dogs run after one dog,
what time is it?
Twenty after one.

So you are distantly related to the
family next door, are you?
Yes – their dog is our dog's
brother.

What do you get if you cross a
centipede with a parrot?
A walkie-talkie.

What's your new dog's name?
Dunno – he won't tell me.

Would you like to play with our new
dog?
He looks very fierce. Does he bite?
That's what I want to find out.

Sign in shop window: FOR SALE
Pedigree bulldog. House trained.
Eats anything. Very fond of
children.

"Why are you crying, little boy?"
" 'Cos we've just had to have our dog put down!" sobbed the lad.
"Was he mad?" asked the old lady.
"Well he wasn't too happy about it."

Jake: That ointment the vet gave me for the dog makes my fingers smart.
Blake: Why don't you rub some on your head then?

How do you know you are haunted
by a parrot?
He keeps saying "ooooo's a pretty
boy then?"

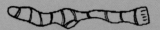

What happened when a doctor
crossed a parrot with a vampire?
It bit his neck, sucked his blood
and said, "Who's a pretty boy
then?"

What is small, smelly and gray,
sucks blood and eats cheese?
A mouse-quito.

What's the name of the opera
about a mouse and a flea?
Der Fleadermouse.

What is the definition of a narrow
squeak?
A thin mouse.

What's the hardest part about milking a mouse?
Getting the bucket underneath it.

Jim: Our dog is just like one of the family.
Fred: Which one?

Which mouse was a Roman
emperor?
Julius Cheeser.

Who is the king of all the mice?
Mouse Tse Tung.

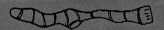

What do angry rodents send each
other at Christmas?
Cross mouse cards.

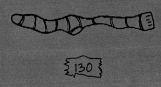

What goes "eek, eek, bang"?
A mouse in a minefield.

What is gray and hairy and lives on
a man's face?
A mousetache.

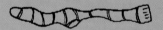

What's gray and furry on the
inside and white on the outside?
A mouse sandwich.

What do you call a mouse that can pick up a monster?
Sir.

How do mice celebrate when they move house?
With a mouse-warming party.

What did the mouse say when his friend broke his front teeth?
Hard cheese.

Why did the mouse eat a candle?
For light refreshment.

What is a mouse's favorite game?
Hide and squeak.

What goes "dot, dot, dash, squeak"?
Mouse code.

What is a mouse's favorite record?
"Please cheese me."

How do you save a drowning rodent?
Use mouse to mouse resuscitation.

What kind of musical instrument
do rats play?
Mouse organ.

Why did the witch keep turning
people into Mickey Mouse?
She was having Disney spells.

Why did the wizard turn the
naughty girl into a mouse?
Because she ratted on him.

First Mouse: I've trained that crazy science teacher at last.
Second Mouse: How have you done that?
First Mouse: I don't know how, but every time I run through that maze and ring the bell, he gives me a piece of cheese.

Why did Mickey Mouse take a trip to outer space?
He wanted to find Pluto.

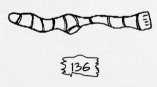

What comes after cheese?
A mouse.

What do you get if you cross King
Kong with a budgie?
A messy cage.

My budgie lays square eggs.
That's amazing! Can it talk as
well?
Yes, but only one word.
What's that?
Ouch!

Not Very Smelly
but Very Creepy!

Mommy monster: Did you catch everyone's eyes in that dress dear?

Girl monster: Yes, mom, and I've brought them all home for Cedric to play marbles with.

What do bats sing when it's raining?

"Raindrops keep falling on my feet."

Doctor, doctor, I keep thinking I'm a
caterpillar.
Don't worry, you'll soon change.

What does a cat go to sleep on?
A caterpillar.

What's green and dangerous?
A caterpillar with a hand-grenade.

What does a caterpillar do on New Year's Day?
Turns over a new leaf.

What has stripes and pulls a tractor?
A caterpillar tractor.

What's the definition of a caterpillar?
A worm in a fur coat.

What's the difference between a maggot and a cockroach? Cockroaches crunch more when you eat them.

What did one maggot say to the other who was stuck in an apple? "Worm your way out of that one, then!"

What's the maggot army called? The apple corps.

What's yellow, wiggly and dangerous?
A maggot with a bad attitude.

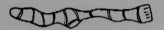

What's worse than finding a maggot in your apple?
Finding half a maggot in your apple.

What did one maggot say to another?
"What's a nice girl like you doing in a joint like this?"

Did you hear about the maggot that was shut up in Tutankhamun's Tomb?
It had a phar-old time.

Where do you find giant snails?
On the end of a giant's fingers.

Knock knock.
Who's there?
Maggot.
Maggot who?
Maggot me this new dress today.

Waiter, waiter, there's a maggot in my salad.
Don't worry, he won't live long in that stuff.

What is the strongest animal in
the world?
A snail, because it carries its home
on its back.

What do you do when two snails
have a fight?
Leave them to slug it out.

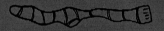

What is the definition of a slug?
A snail with a housing problem.

What was the snail doing on the highway?
About one mile a day.

How do snails get their shells all shiny?
They use snail varnish.

What gas do snails prefer?
Shell.

How did the clever snail carry his home?
He used a snail-trailer.

What do you get if you cross Dracula with a snail?
The world's slowest vampire.

Doctor, doctor, I keep thinking I'm a snail.
Don't worry, we'll soon have you out of your shell.

Waiter, waiter, do you serve snails.
Sit down, sir, we'll serve anyone.

What is a snail?
A slug with a crash helmet.

What creepie crawlies do athletes break?
Tapeworms.

What do worms leave round their bathtubs?
The scum of the earth.

Waiter, waiter, are there snails on the menu?
Oh yes, sir, they must have escaped from the kitchen.

Why didn't the two worms go into Noah's ark in an apple?
Because everyone had to go in pairs.

How do you make a glowworm happy?
Cut off its tail. It'll be de-lighted.

What is the glowworms' favorite song?
"Wake Me Up Before You Glow Glow" by Wham!

What do you get if you cross a
worm with a young goat?
A dirty kid.

What do you get if you cross a
glowworm with a pint of beer?
Light ale.

How can you tell which end of a
worm is its head?
Tickle its middle and see which
end smiles.

Why was the glowworm unhappy?
Because her children were not very bright.

What did the woodworm say to the chair?
It's been nice gnawing you!

One worm said to the other "I love you, I love you, I love you."
"Don't be stupid," the other worm said, "I'm your other end!"

When should you stop for a
glowworm?
When he has a red light.

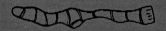

How can you tell if you are looking
at a police glowworm?
He has a blue light.

Why are glowworms good to carry
in your bag?
They can lighten your load.

What do you call an amorous
insect?
The Love Bug.

What do you call an insect that has
just flown by?
A flu bug.

Which fly makes films?
Stephen Spielbug.

What do you call a nervous insect?
Jitterbug.

Who stole the sheets of the bed?
Bed buglars.

What do you say to an annoying
cockroach?
"Stop bugging me!"

What do you call an insect from
outer space?
Bug Rogers.

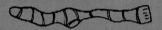

What do you get if you cross a
praying mantis with a termite?
A bug that says grace before
eating your house.

Why was the insect kicked out of
the park?
It was a litterbug.

What do you call singing insects?
Humbugs.

What did one insect say to the other?
Stop bugging me.

Insect Films: The Fly; Batman; Beatlejuice; The Sting; The Good, the Bug and the Ugly; Spawn; The Frog Prince; Four Webbings and a Funeral; Seven Bats for Seven Brothers.

Knock knock.
Who's there?
Bug.
Bug who?
Bugsy Malone.

Doctor, doctor, I keep seeing an
insect spinning round.
Don't worry, it's just a bug that's
going round.

Doctor, doctor, I keep dreaming there are great, gooey, bug-eyed monsters playing tiddleywinks under my bed. What shall I do?
Hide the tiddleywinks.

What do you get if you cross a flea with a rabbit?
A bug's bunny.

What did one worm say to another when he was late home?
Why in earth are you late?

What's the difference between a worm and a gooseberry?
Ever tried eating worm pie?

What is the best advice to give a worm?
Sleep late.

Why did the sparrow fly into the library?
It was looking for bookworms.

What lives in apples and is an avid reader?
A bookworm.

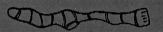

One woodworm met another.
"How's life?" she asked.
"Oh, same as usual," he replied, "boring."

What do you call a rich frog?
A gold-blooded reptile.

How do frogs manage to lay so many eggs?
They sit eggsaminations.

What do headmasters and bullfrogs have in common?
Both have a big head that consists mostly of mouth.

What kind of bull doesn't have horns?
A bullfrog.

What jumps up and down in front
of a car?
Froglights.

Where does a ten-ton frog sleep?
Anywhere it wants to!

When is a car like a frog?
When it's being toad.

What did one frog say to the
other?
Time's sure fun when you're
having flies!

What did the bus conductor say to
the frog?
"Hop on."

What do you say to a hitchhiking
frog?
"Hop in!"

Why did the toad become a
lighthouse keeper?
He had his own frog-horn.

What happened when the frog
joined the cricket team?
He bowled long hops.

What do you get if you cross a frog
with a ferry?
A hoppercraft.

What do you call a frog who wants
to be a cowboy?
Hoppalong Cassidy.

Why do frogs have webbed feet?
To stamp out forest fires.

What do frogs sit on?
Toadstools.

What happens to illegally parked frogs?
They get toad away.

What's green and can jump a mile a minute?
A frog with hiccups.

What did the croaking frog say to his friend?
"I think I've got a person in my throat."

What's green and goes round and round at 60 miles an hour?
A frog in a liquidizer.

What is yellow and goes round and round at 60 miles an hour?
A mouldy frog in a liquidizer.

What is a frog's favorite game?
Croak-et.

What is a frog's favorite flower?
The croakus.

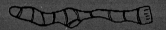

What is green and slimy and is
found at the North Pole?
A lost frog.

Where do frogs keep their
treasure?
In a croak of gold at the end of the
rainbow.

What do frogs drink?
Hot croako.

What kind of shoes do frogs like?
Open-toad sandals.

What do you call a frog spy?
A croak and dagger agent.

What do you call an eighty-year-
old frog?
An old croak.

What do you call a girl with a frog
on her head?
Lily.

What's white on the outside, green
on the inside and comes with
relish and onions?
A hot frog.

What happens if you eat a hot
frog?
You croak in no time.

Where do you get frogs' eggs?
In a spawn shop.

Why didn't the female frog lay
eggs?
Because her husband spawned
her affections.

Why didn't the witch sing at the concert?
Because she had a frog in her throat.

Collecting Reptiles – by Ivor Frog

What do you get if you cross a werewolf with a frog?
A creature that can bite you from the other side of the road.

What goes "croak, croak" when it's foggy?
A frog-horn.

Waiter, waiter, there's a frog in my soup.
Well I'll tell him to hop it.

Doctor, doctor, I think I'm turning into a frog.
Oh, you're just playing too much croquet.

Knock knock.
Who's there?
Crispin.
Crispin who?
Crispin crunchy frog sandwich.

Waiter, waiter, do you have frogs'
legs?
Yes, Sir.
Well then hop into the kitchen for
my soup.

Doctor, doctor, I keep thinking I'm a frog.
What's wrong with that?
I think I'm going to croak.

Waiter, waiter, have you got frogs' legs?
No, Sir, I always walk like this.

Waiter, waiter, can I have frogs' legs?
Well I suppose you could but you'd need surgery!

What do you call an ant with frog's legs?
An ant-phibian.

What do frogs drink?
Croaka Cola.

What is a bookworm's idea of a big feast?
War and Peace.

What would you do if you found a bookworm chewing your favorite book?
Take the words right out of its mouth.

What do clever bookworms win?
The Booker Prize.

What do you get if you cross an anaconda with a glowworm?
A thirty-foot strip light.

Collecting Wriggly Creatures – by Tina Worms.

What did one glowworm say to another when his light went out? "Give me a push, my battery is dead."

Fisherman: What are you fishing for sonny?
Boy: I'm not fishing, I'm drowning worms.

First man: My wife eats like a bird.
Second man: You mean she hardly
eats a thing?
First man: No, she eats slugs and
worms.

Surveyor: This house is a ruin. I
wonder what stops it from falling
down.
Owner: I think the woodworm are
holding hands.

Did you hear about the stupid woodworm?
He was found in a brick.

Did you hear about the glowworm that didn't know if it was coming or glowing?

How do you keep flies out of the kitchen?
Put a bucket of manure in the lounge.

Doctor, doctor, I feel like an
insignificant worm.
Next!

Waiter, waiter, there are two worms
on my plate.
Those are your sausages, sir.

How do fireflies start a race?
"Ready, steady, glow!"

Time flies like an arrow, but fruit flies like a banana.

If there are five flies in the kitchen, which one is the American football player?
The one in the sugar bowl.

What wears a black cape, flies through the night and sucks blood?
A mosquito in a cape.

Why were the flies playing football
in a saucer?
They were playing for the cup.

What has four wheels and flies?
A garbage bin.

What did the slug say as he
slipped down the window very
fast?
"How slime flies!"

What has six legs and flies?
A witch giving her cat a lift.

Waiter, waiter, there are two flies in
my soup.
That's all right sir. Have the extra
one on me.

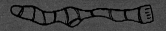

What happens to a witch when she
loses her temper riding her
broomstick?
She flies off the handle.

What has handles and flies?
A witch in a garbage bin.

Boy: My sister's the school swot.
Girl: Does she do well in exams.
Boy: No, but she kills a lot of flies.

Waiter, waiter, what's this
cockroach doing in my soup?
We ran out of flies.

Waiter, waiter, there's a dead fly swimming in my soup.
Nonsense sir, dead flies can't swim.

Doctor, doctor, I don't like all these flies buzzing around my head.
Pick out the ones you like and I'll swat the rest.

Two flies were on a cereal packet.
"Why are we running so fast?"
asked one.
"Because," said the second, "it
says 'tear along the dotted line'!"

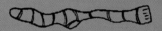

Teacher: If I had ten flies on my
desk, and I swatted one, how many
flies would be left?
Girl: One – the dead one!

Pungent
Pongs

Did you hear the joke about the skunk?
Never mind, it stinks!

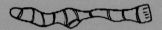

What do you get if you cross a skunk with a boomerang?
A bad smell you can't get rid of.

Scotty: I say, I say, I say, my dog's got no nose!
Snotty: How does he smell?
Scotty: Terrible!

What do you get if you cross a skunk with a porcupine?
A smelly pincushion.

Did you hear about the dog that ate garlic?
His bark was worse than his bite.

What did one sardine say to the other sardine when he saw a submarine?
"There goes a can full of people."

What do guests do at a cannibal wedding?
They toast the bride and groom.

Why did the cannibal have a bad stomach?
Because he ate people who disagreed with him.

What did the vegetarian cannibal eat?
Swedes.

What kind of girl does a mummy
take on a date?
Any old girl he can dig up.

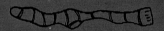

Why did the cannibal feel sick
after eating the missionary?
Because you can't keep a good
man down.

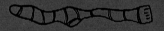

What kind of aftershave do
monsters wear?
Brute.

Did you hear about the plastic surgeon?
He sat in front of the fire and melted.

"I wouldn't say he was filthy, but his clothes get dirtier on the inside than on the outside."

"Mommy, Mommy, Why can't we have a garbage bin?"
"Shut up and keep chewing."

I wouldn't say Basil was insensitive, but he did walk into a crematorium and ask what was cooking!

Stinker: I know a café where we can eat dirt cheap.
Pongo: But who wants to eat dirt?

Waiter: Soup's off today, sir.
Diner: I'll say it is. Mine had green mould on it.

What does a professor of anatomy
eat with cheese?
Pickled organs.

Why did the orchestra player live
on baked beans?
So he could play the Trumpet
Voluntary.

Did you hear the joke about the
three eggs?
Two bad.

Waiter, what's wrong with this fish?
Long time, no sea, sir.

Knock, knock.
Who's there?
Kipper.
Kipper who?
Kipper your hands to yourself.

What's the dirtiest word in the world?
Pollution.

What's brown and sounds like a
bell?
Dung.

Mr Stench, peering over garden
fence: What are you going to do
with that pile of manure?
Mr Pong: Put it on my
strawberries.
Mr Stench: Really? I put cream on
mine.

Why was the silly man expelled
from the committee meeting?
He passed the wrong sort of
motion.

What has two legs, one wheel, and
stinks to high heaven?
A barrowload of manure.

Did you hear about the posh school
where all the pupils smelled?
It was for filthy rich kids only.

Doctor: I can't diagnose the cause of your bad breath. I think it must be the drink.
Patient: OK, I'll come back when you're sober.

Did you hear about the man who had B.O. on one side only?
He bought Right Guard, but couldn't find any Left Guard.

"Do you know," said the teacher to one of her pupils who had B.O., "that we call you the wonder child in the staffroom?"
"Why's that, Miss?"
"Because we all wonder when you're going to wash!"

Doctor, doctor, these pills you gave me for B.O . . .
What's wrong with them?
They keep slipping from under my arms!

Do you always talk like that or are you wearing itchy underwear?

Knock knock.
Who's there?
Underwear.
Underwear who?
Underwear my baby is tonight?

Why is perfume obedient?
Because it is scent wherever it goes.

My sister is so stupid she thinks
that aroma is someone who travels
a lot.

What do you get if you cross a
vampire with a rose?
A flower that goes for your throat
when you sniff it.

What's yellow and sniffs?
A banana with a bad cold.

How many drops of acetic acid
does it take to make a stink bomb?
Quite a phew.

Did you hear about the little man
who thought he was Dracula?
He was a pain in the bum.

Why is a man wearing sunglasses
like a rotten teacher?
Because he keeps his pupils in the
dark.

What has a bottom at the top?
I don't know.
Your legs.

What comes out at night and goes
"Munch, munch, ouch"?
A vampire with a rotten tooth.

Chased by a Werewolf – by Claude Bottom.

What's the name for a short-legged tramp?
A low-down bum.

Which two letters are rotten for your teeth?
D K.

How do you stop a skunk from smelling?
Fix a clothes peg to its nose.

What's purple and hums?
A rotten plum!

What did the cat do after it had swallowed the cheese?
Waited at the mousehole with baited beath.

What smells most in the zoo?
Your nose.

What's the difference between
school dinners and a bucket of
fresh manure?
School dinners are usually cold.

What's the difference between a skunk and a mouse?
A skunk uses a cheaper deodorant.

Why did the skunk buy six boxes of paper handkerchiefs?
Because he had a stinking cold.

What did the skunk say when the wind changed from west to east?
"It's all coming back to me now."

What do you get if you cross a
young goat with a pig?
A dirty kid.

Why do giraffes have such long
necks?
Because their feet smell.

Why do people keep away from
bats?
Because of their bat breath.

Ordinary Odors

What happens if you cross a
piranha fish with a rose?
I don't know, but I wouldn't try
smelling it.

Knock, knock.
Who's there?
Paul Aidy.
Paul Aidy who?
Paul Aidy, Stinker just pushed her
over in the mud.

Pongo: I think my mom's trying to get rid of me. Every time she wraps up my packed lunch she puts a road map in it.

Who lived in the woods and told dirty jokes to wolves?
Little Rude Riding Hood.

Why did the millionaire live in a mansion without a bathroom?
He was filthy rich.

What is an ig?
An Eskimo house without a loo.

What did the speak-your-weight
machine say when the large lady
stepped on it?
"One at a time, please."

Did you hear about the girl who
bought a pair of paper knickers?
She didn't like them; they were
tear-able.

Knock, knock.
Who's there?
Euripides.
Euripides who?
Euripides you pay for a new pair.

Knock, knock.
Who's there?
Nick.
Nick who?
Nick R. Elastic.

She stood on the bridge at
midnight,
Her lips were all a-quiver.
She gave a cough, her leg fell off,
And floated down the river.

"Dad, are you sure it's true that we
are made of dust?"
"Yes, son."
"Then how come I don't get muddy
when I go swimming?"

Boy: Dad, dad, there's a spider in the bath.
Dad: What wrong with that? You've seen spiders before.
Boy: yes, but this one is three feet wide and using all the hot water!

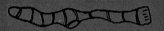

What did the headless horseman say when someone gave him a comb?
"I will never part with this."

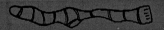

How do you communicate with the Loch Ness Monster at 20,000 fathoms?
Drop him a line.

"Alec," said the religious education teacher, "you've written here that Samson was an actor. What makes you think that?"
"Well Sir," said Alec, "I read that he brought the house down."

What's the longest piece of
furniture in the school?
The multiplication table.

How do Religious Education
teachers mark exams?
With spirit levels.

Why did the old lady cover her
mouth with her hands when she
sneezed?
To catch her false teeth.

How did the Vikings communicate
with one another?
By Norse code.

"Doctor Sawbones speaking."
"Oh, doctor, my wife's just
dislocated her jaw. Can you come
over in, say, three or four weeks
time?"

Teacher: Tommy Russell, you're late again.

Tommy: Sorry, sir. It's my bus – it's always coming late.

Teacher: Well, if it's late again tomorrow, catch an earlier one.

Knock knock.
Who's there?
Tristan.
Tristan who?
Tristan insect to really get up your nose.

Paddy and Mick were sent to jail in a high security prison, but they developed an ingenious method of communicating with each other by means of a secret code and banging on the pipes. However, their scheme broke down when they were transferred to different cells.

Waiter, waiter, there's a fly in my soup!
Don't worry, sir, the spider in the butter will catch it.

Father: How did the greenhouse get smashed?
Arthur: I was cleaning my catapult and it went off.

What did the mommy snake say to the crying baby snake?
"Stop crying and viper your nose."

Why didn't the viper, viper nose?
Because the adder adder handkerchief.

How do you know when there's a
monster under your bed?
Your nose touches the ceiling.

Why did the monster have green
ears and a red nose?
So that he could hide in rhubarb
patches.

What usually runs in witches'
families?
Noses.

What happened to the witch with
an upside down nose?
Every time she sneezed her hat
blew off.

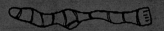

There was a big monster from
Leek
Who, instead of a nose, had a
beak.
It grew quite absurd
Till he looked like a bird.
He migrates at the end of next
week.

Wizard: You've got a Roman nose.

Witch: Like Julius Caesar?

Wizard: No, it's roamin' all over your face.

Monster: Doctor, doctor, how do I stop my nose from running?

Doctor: Stick out your foot and trip it up.

What's the difference between a bus driver and a cold in the head? A bus driver knows the stops, and a cold in the head stops the nose.

Werewolf: Doctor, doctor, thank you so much for curing me.

Doctor: So you don't think you're a werewolf anymore?

Werewolf: Absolutely not, I'm quite clear now – see my nose is nice and cold.

Witch: Doctor, I've got a head like a turnip, three ears, two noses and a mouth the wrong way round. What am I?

Doctor: Ugly

Why did the teacher have her hair
in a bun?
Because she had her nose in a
hamburger.

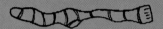

Why did the monster take his nose
apart?
To see what made it run.

What do you do if your nose goes
on strike?
Picket.

Did you hear about Lenny the Loafer?
He is so lazy that he sticks his nose out of the window so that the wind will blow it for him.

What's the difference between a Peeping Tom and someone who's just got out of the bath?
One is rude and nosey. The other is nude and rosey.

Did you hear about the boy who got worried when his nose grew to eleven inches long?
He thought it might turn into a foot.

What is it that even the most careful person overlooks?
His nose.

How did the monkey make toast?
He put it under the gorilla.

Visitor: You're very quiet, Jennifer.
Jennifer: Well, my mom gave me 10 cents not to say anything about your red nose.

"You boy!" called a policeman.
"Can you help? We're looking for a
man with a huge red nose called
Cotters . . ."
"Really?" said the boy. "What're
his ears called?"

Doctor, doctor, every time I drink a
cup of tea I get a sharp pain in my
nose.
Have you tried taking the spoon
out of the cup?

"Why's your son crying?" the doctor asked a young woman in his surgery.

"He has four baked beans stuck up his nose."

"And why's his little sister screaming?"

"She wants the rest of her lunch back."

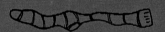

Why do grape harvesters have noses?

So they have something to pick during the growing season.

Did you hear about the man who was so stupid that when he picked his nose he tore the lining of his hat?

"I see the baby's nose is running again," said a worried father. "For goodness sake!" snapped his wife. "Can't you think of anything apart from racing?"

Simon: I was going to buy you a handkerchief for your birthday.

Sarah: That was a kind thought. But why didn't you?

Simon: I couldn't find one big enough for your nose.

Which villains steal soap from the bath?

Robber ducks.

When the school was broken into, the thieves took absolutely everything – desks, books, blackboards, everything apart from the soap in the lavatories and all the towels. The police are looking for a pair of dirty criminals.

Why did the stupid sailor grab a bar of soap when his ship sank? He thought he could wash himself ashore.

Doctor: And did you drink your medicine after your bath, Mrs Soap?

Mrs Soap: No, Doctor. By the time I'd drunk the bath there wasn't room for medicine.

Brian: Our school must have very clean kitchens.

Bill: How can you tell?

Brian: All the food tastes of soap.

How did your mom know you hadn't washed your face?
I forgot to wet the soap.

Mrs Brown was always complaining about her husband. "If things go on like this I'll have to leave him," she moaned to Mrs Jenkins.
"Give him the soft-soap treatment," said Mrs Jenkins.
"I tried that," replied Mrs Brown, "it didn't work. He spotted it at the top of the stairs."

School meals are not generally popular with those that have to eat them, and sometimes with good reason.

"What kind of pie do you call this?" asked one schoolboy indignantly.

"What's it taste of?" asked the cook.

"Glue!"

"Then it's apple pie – the plum pie tastes of soap."

This morning my dad gave me
soap flakes instead of corn flakes
for breakfast!
I bet you were mad.
Mad? I was foaming at the mouth!

Mom, will you wash my face?
Why can't you wash it yourself?
'Cos that'll mean my hands
getting wet, and they don't need
washing!

I hear he's a very careful person.
Well, he likes to economize on soap
and water.

What happened when the werewolf
fell in the washing machine?
He became a wash-and-werewolf.

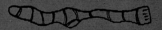

Why did the burglar steal a
washing machine?
He wanted to make a clean
getaway.

Why did the witch put her broom in the washing machine?
She wanted a clean sweep.

What does a black mamba do in the toilet?
Tries to wash his hands.

Girl: Mom, mom a monster's just bitten my foot off.
Mom: Well keep out of the kitchen, I've just washed the floor.

Do you look in the mirror after you've washed?
No, I look in the towel!

That boy is so dirty, the only time he washes his ears is when he eats watermelon.

Teacher: What's the difference between a buffalo and a bison?
Student: You can't wash your hands in a buffalo, Miss.

Anne: Ugh! The water in my glass is cloudy.
Dan, trying to impress his new girlfriend: It's all right, it's just that the glass hasn't been washed.

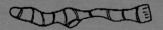

The dirty old tramp sidled up to a passerby. "Got a dollar for a bed for the night?" he muttered.

"No," said the passer by firmly.

"Got 50 cents for a meal?"

"Certainly not."

"Oh . . . have you got 20 cents for a cup of tea, then?"

"No, I have not."

"Blimey – you'd better take my mouth organ. You're worse off than I am."

On their first evening in their new home the bride went in to the kitchen to fix the drinks. Five minutes later she came back into the living room in tears. "What's the matter, my angel?" asked her husband anxiously.

"Oh Derek!" she sobbed. "I put the ice cubes in hot water to wash them and they've disappeared!"

Sign in a launderette: Those using automatic washers should remove their clothes when the lights go out.

"What steps would you take," roared the sergeant instructor, "if one of the enemy came at you with a bayonet?"
A small voice in the rear rank muttered, "Dirty great big ones!"

A man sitting in a barber's chair noticed that the barber's hands were very dirty. When he commented on this, the barber explained,
"Yes, Sir, no one's been in for a shampoo yet."